BACKYARD TIGERS
(VOLUME 2)

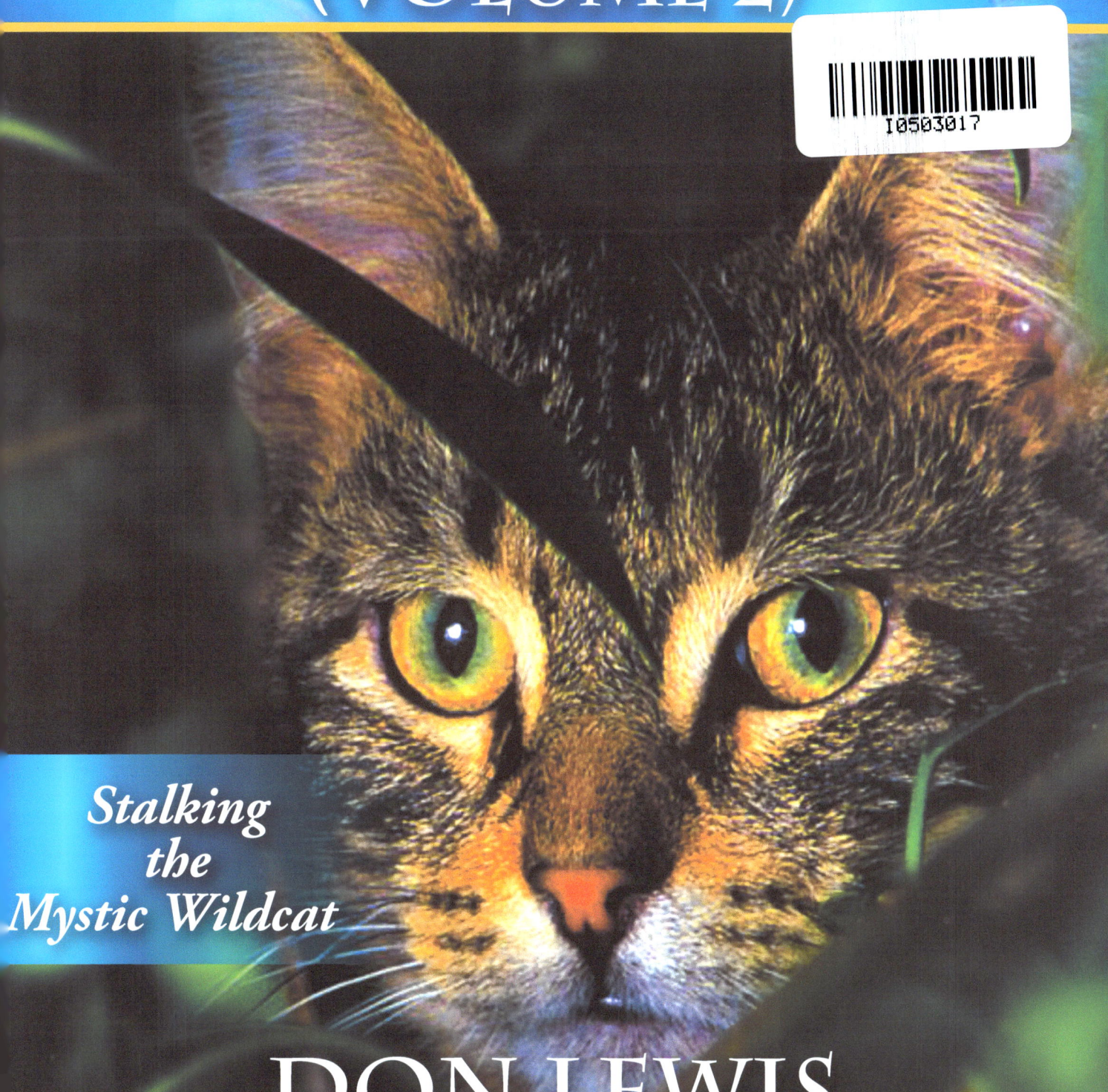

I0503017

*Stalking
the
Mystic Wildcat*

DON LEWIS

Copyright © 2013 by Don Lewis. 136857-LEWI

ISBN: Softcover   978-1-4836-5417-1
          Ebook   978-1-4836-5418-8

All rights reserved. No part of this book may
be reproduced or transmitted in any form or by
any means, electronic or mechanical, including
photocopying, recording, or by any information
storage and retrieval system, without permission in
writing from the copyright owner.

Rev. date: 07/10/2013

To order additional copies of this book, contact:
Xlibris Corporation
1-888-795-4274
www.Xlibris.com
Orders@Xlibris.com

eldonwes@yahoo.com

INTRODUCTION

To me, there is something engaging in seeing a picture of a cat in a natural setting. It has drama. We weave little scenarios around it. Is the cat hunting? Being hunted? Natural settings seem to emphasize the cat's photogenic qualities.

In our backyard tabbies, it's not difficult to see a reflection of their larger, fearsome cousins. Tabby, fawn, spotted and black are all types of coats that domestic cats share with wild felines.

When photographing cats outdoors, especially in foliage, it is frequently necessary to use electronic flash to supplement the existing light. I usually bounce the flash off a large reflector, creating an illuminated area within the foliage. This method presents a number of problems, the most notable of which - as anyone who has photographed cats knows - is getting the cat to occupy the illuminated area. The key to a successful photograph lies in obtaining a subtle balance between natural and artificial light.

During the winter months, I photograph my cats indoors, using props such as rocks and potted plants to create the appearance of natural settings. When shooting active, elusive subjects such as cats, a certain amount of time spent patiently observing through the viewfinder is a necessity. However, you may find the observing to be an enjoyable activity in itself. As the French writer, Colette, observed, "Time spent with cats is never wasted." So, after a hard day in your backyard jungle, take off your pith helmet, have a gin and tonic and congratulate yourself on having survived a day in the wild with *Felis silvestris catus*.

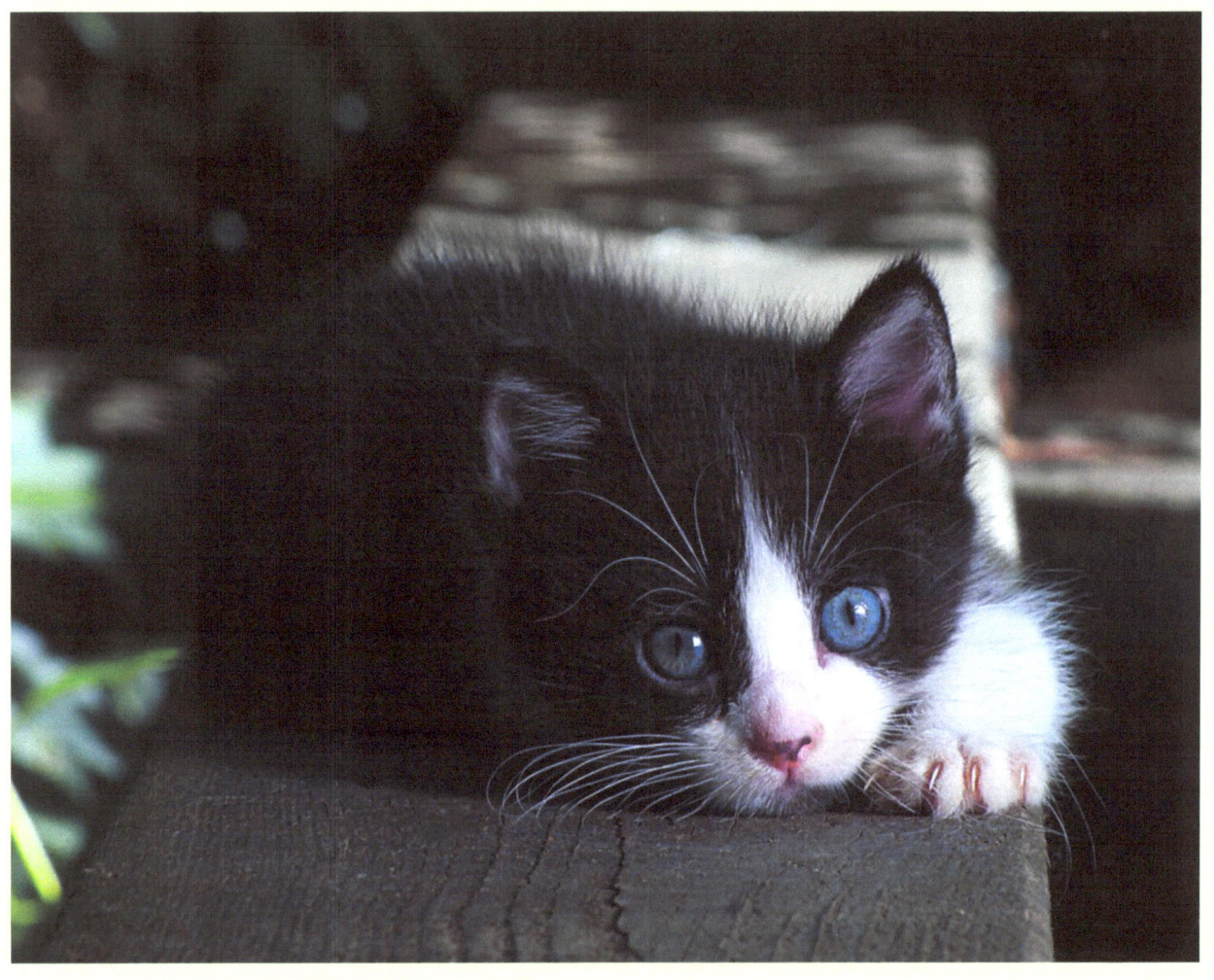

"In general, our modern breeds of cats are doubtless the descendants of wild kittens brought home by prehistoric hunters for their troglodyte children."

The Panther Of The Hearth
National Geographic, 1937

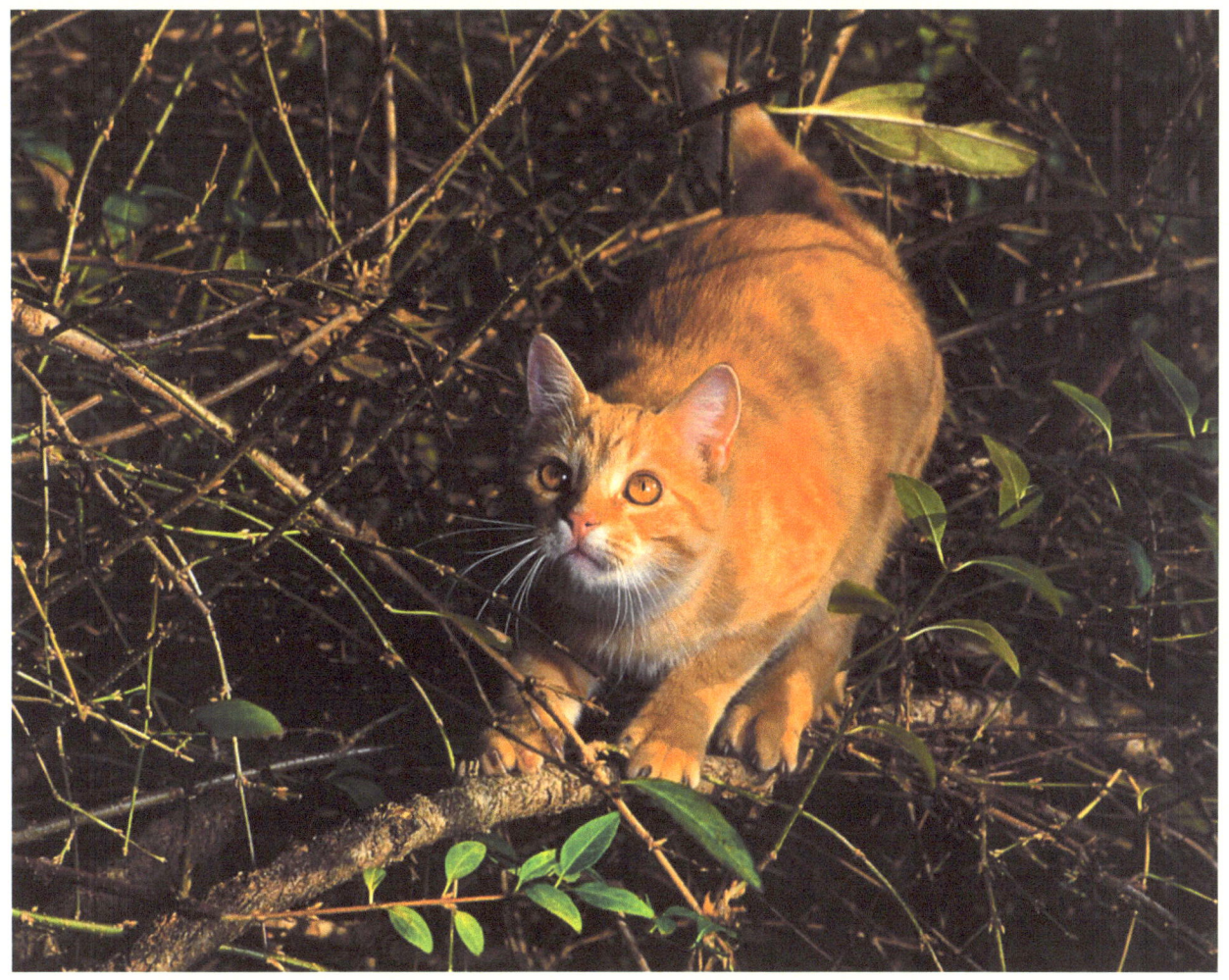

There is something inspiring in the intrepid, resolute way in which a cat goes about its business. A cat in full stealth configuration is a marvel of concentration and impending energy.

A high degree of determination is, of course, something one might expect in an animal that makes its living catching and eating other animals. If the cat has a certain hauteur it is the necessary superiority of the predator over the prey.

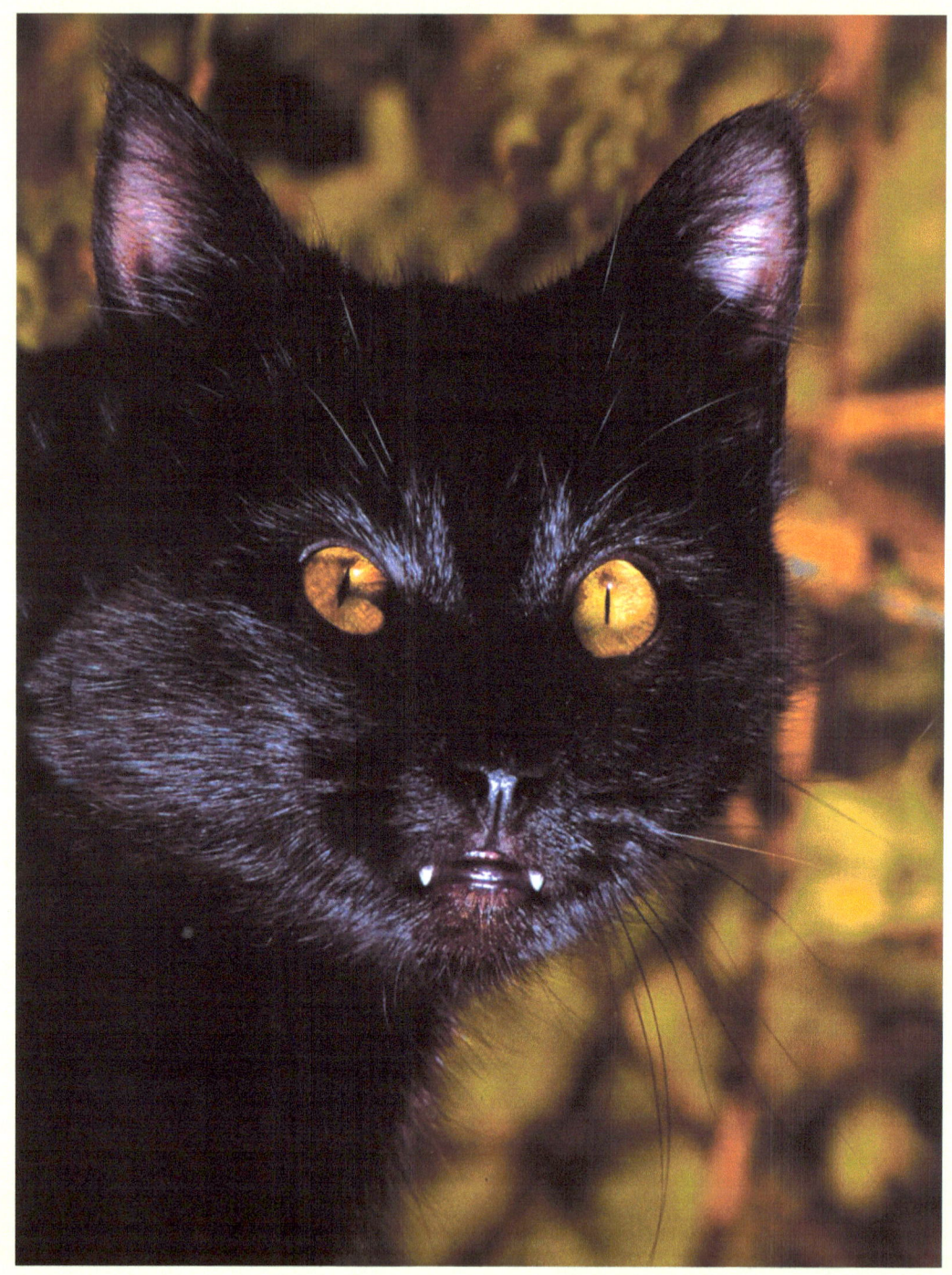

"The cat with his phosphoric eyes, which serve him as lanterns, and sparks flying from his back, fearlessly haunts the darkness, where he encounters wandering phantoms, sorcerers, alchemists, necromancers, resurrectionists, lovers, pickpockets, assassins, drunken patrols, and all those obscene larvae which sally forth and do their work only at night."

Theophile Gautier

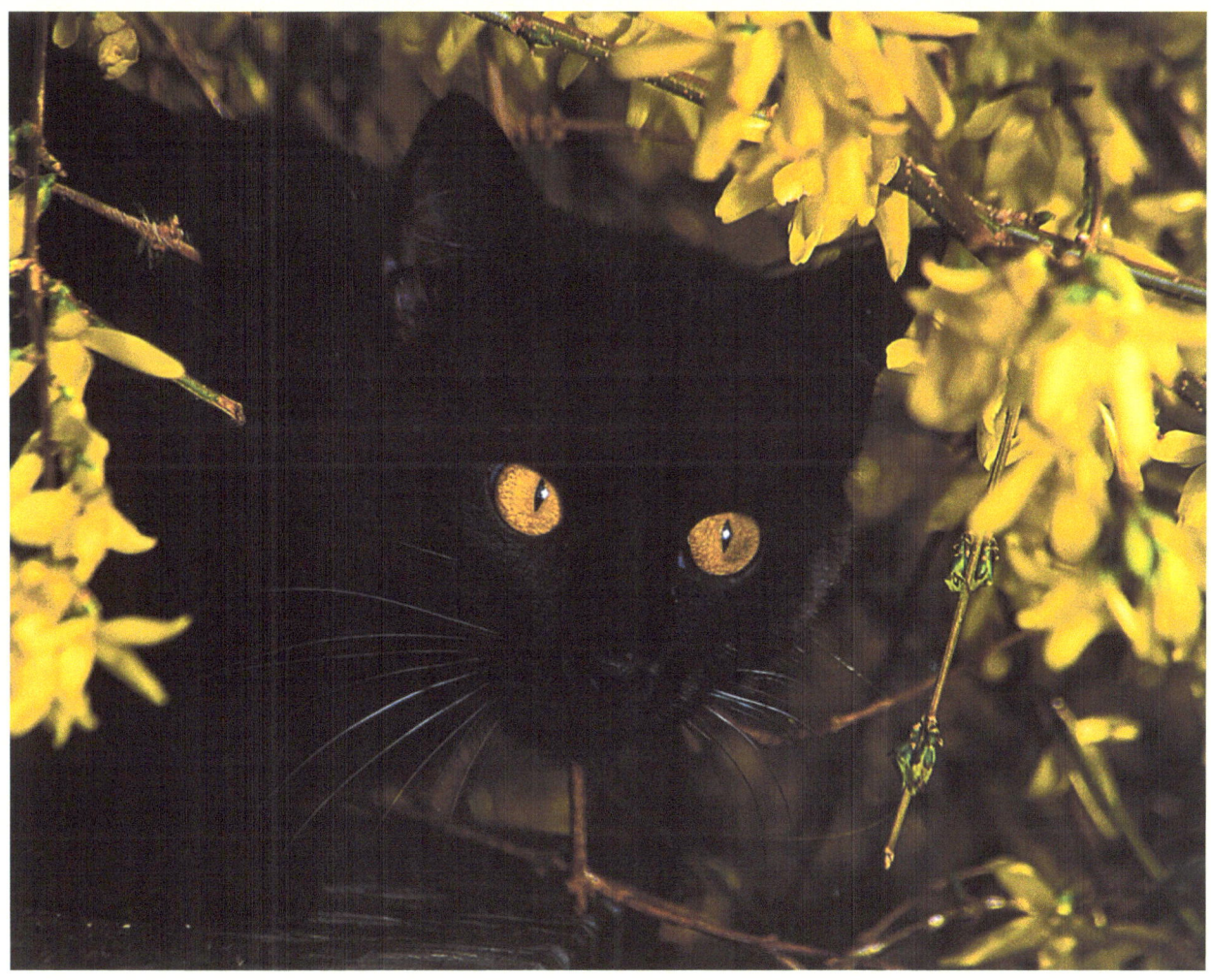

"Animals which symbolized courage and audacity in battle, such as the lion and the leopard, were much featured in heraldry. The image of the cat was also used by families in whose name the sound "cat" or "chat" occurred. The Scottish Chattan clan had a Scottish Wild Cat on its coat-of-arms; the Catesby family had a spotted cat."

Claudia Angeletti
Cats Of The World

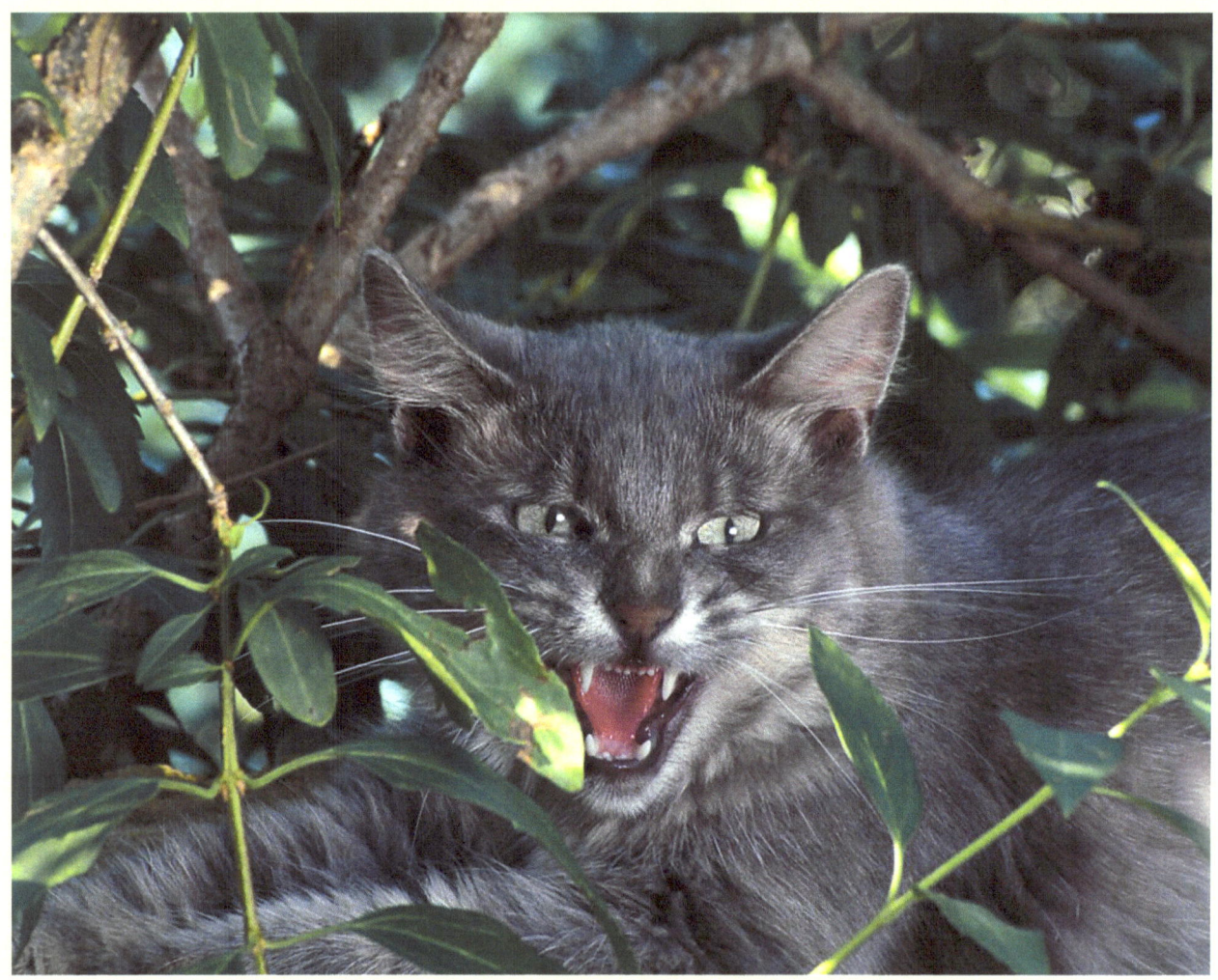

"In Scotland, up to the end of the middle ages, the peasants were authorized to destroy them (the local wildcats) at will and use their fur for clothing. Scottish folklore is full of stories of these cat hunts, which turned into battles and which, in some cases, ended with the cat chasing the man back home. Many of these battles were said to be a fight, between equals, to the death."

John Montgomery
The World Of Cats

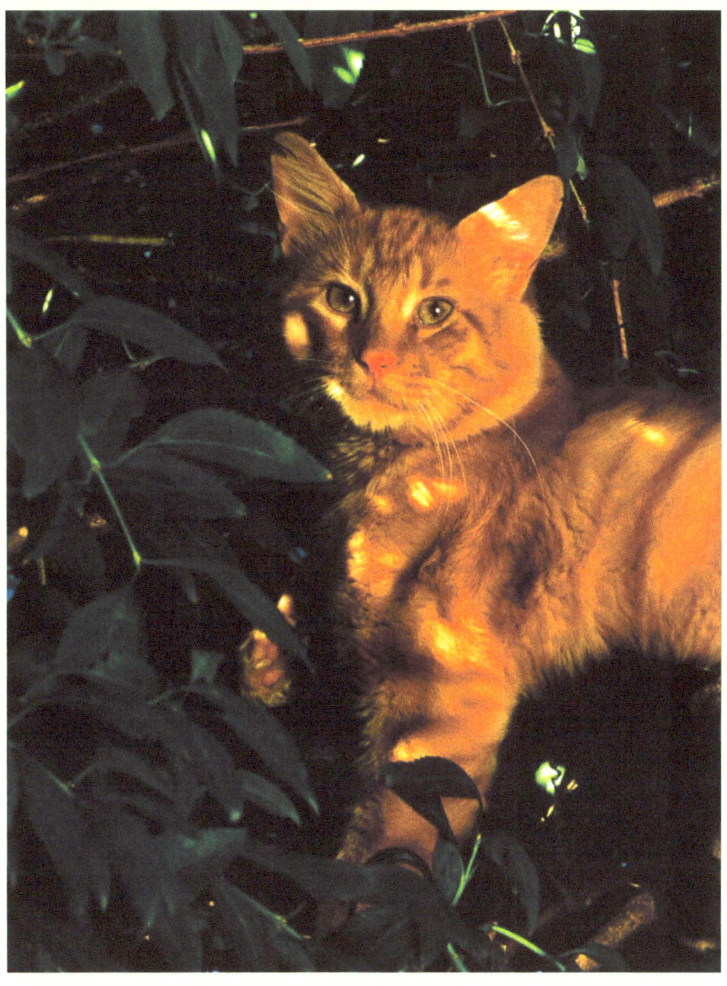

There are numerous stories about cats in the folklore of different cultures. That many of these tales do not say a lot about the cat is obvious since they are often contradictory, i.e., the black cat is considered lucky in some cultures and unlucky in others.

What they are saying is something about the place that the cat occupies in our psychic landscape. No other animal has had such myriad attributes projected upon it. The cat, to be sure, has a grip on our imagination.

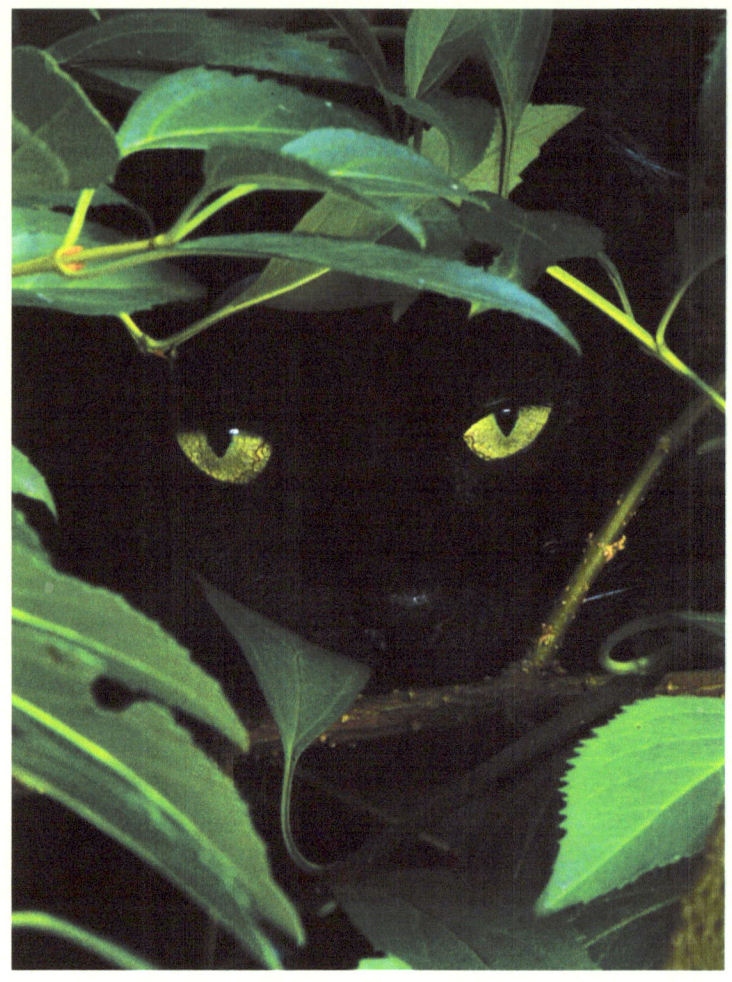

Cats are swift, powerful, stealthy, nocturnal and carnivorous. Small cats are miniature versions of animals of which we humans have an instinctive fear. When we see a cat staring out from the undergrowth, its eyes focused intently, a memory within our collective psyche surfaces and a question occurs. Are we the prey?

"The animals composing this genus (which includes the lion, tiger, panther, etc.) are the most powerful and ferocious of all predatory quadrupeds, as the eagles and birds of prey are among the feathered tribes. ...Their aspect is ferocious, their instincts bloody, and their strength great; even their voice has something in it harsh and terrible."

The American Cyclopaedia, 1881

"In extreme cases fear of cats may become morbid and even be accompanied by typical symptoms of hysteria: paleness, profuse sweating, nausea and profound emotional disturbance, sometimes terminating in fainting."

Encyclopedia Britannica, 1965

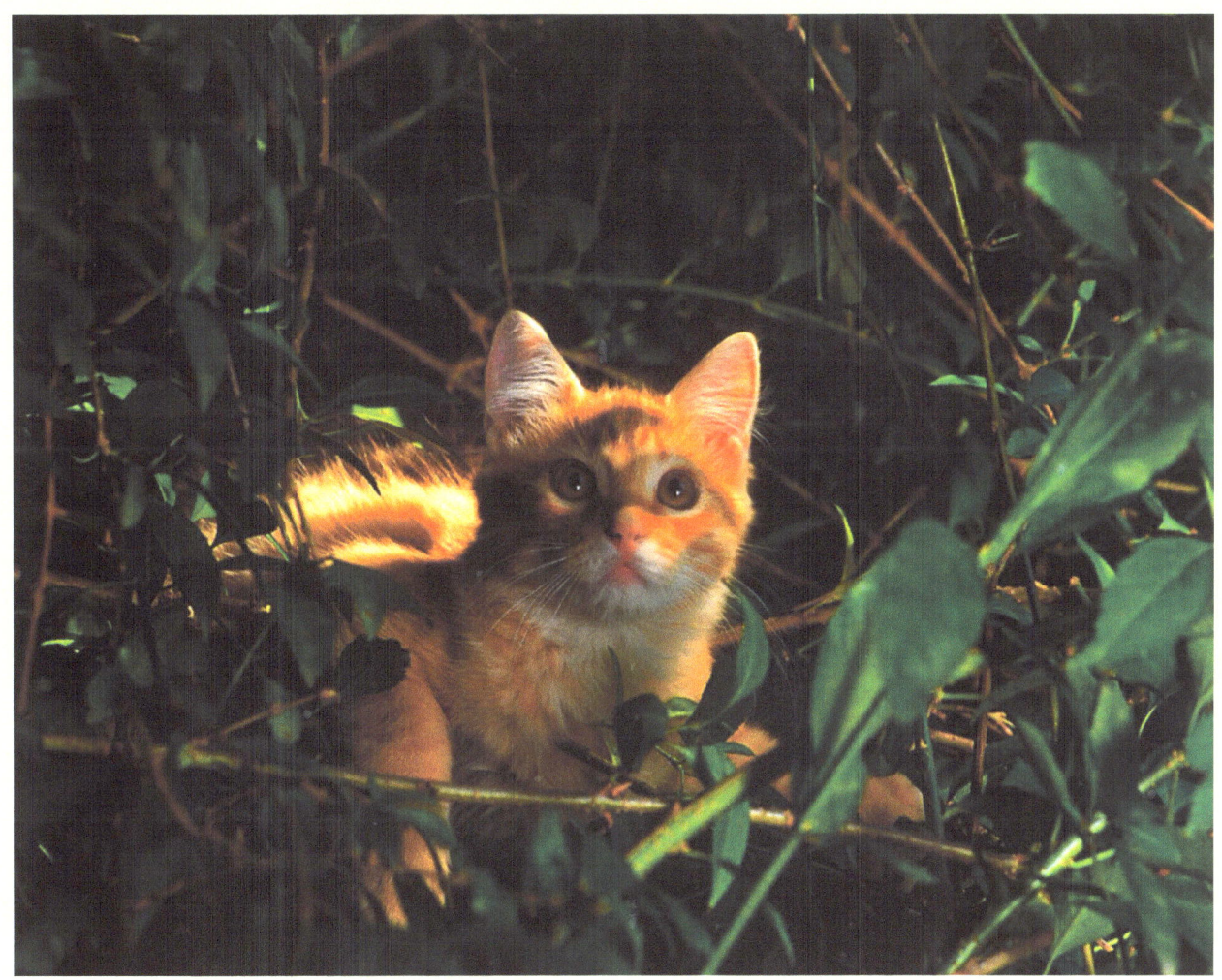

Cats seem to inhabit paradoxical realms: night and day, nature and civilization, ferocity and amiability, the mysterious and the familiar. The typically indolent, congenial household feline goes out at night and becomes transformed, for all intents and purposes, into a wild cat. Stimulated and alert, her senses telling her that she is at home in a world that contains everything she needs, she reverts to her primordial ways.

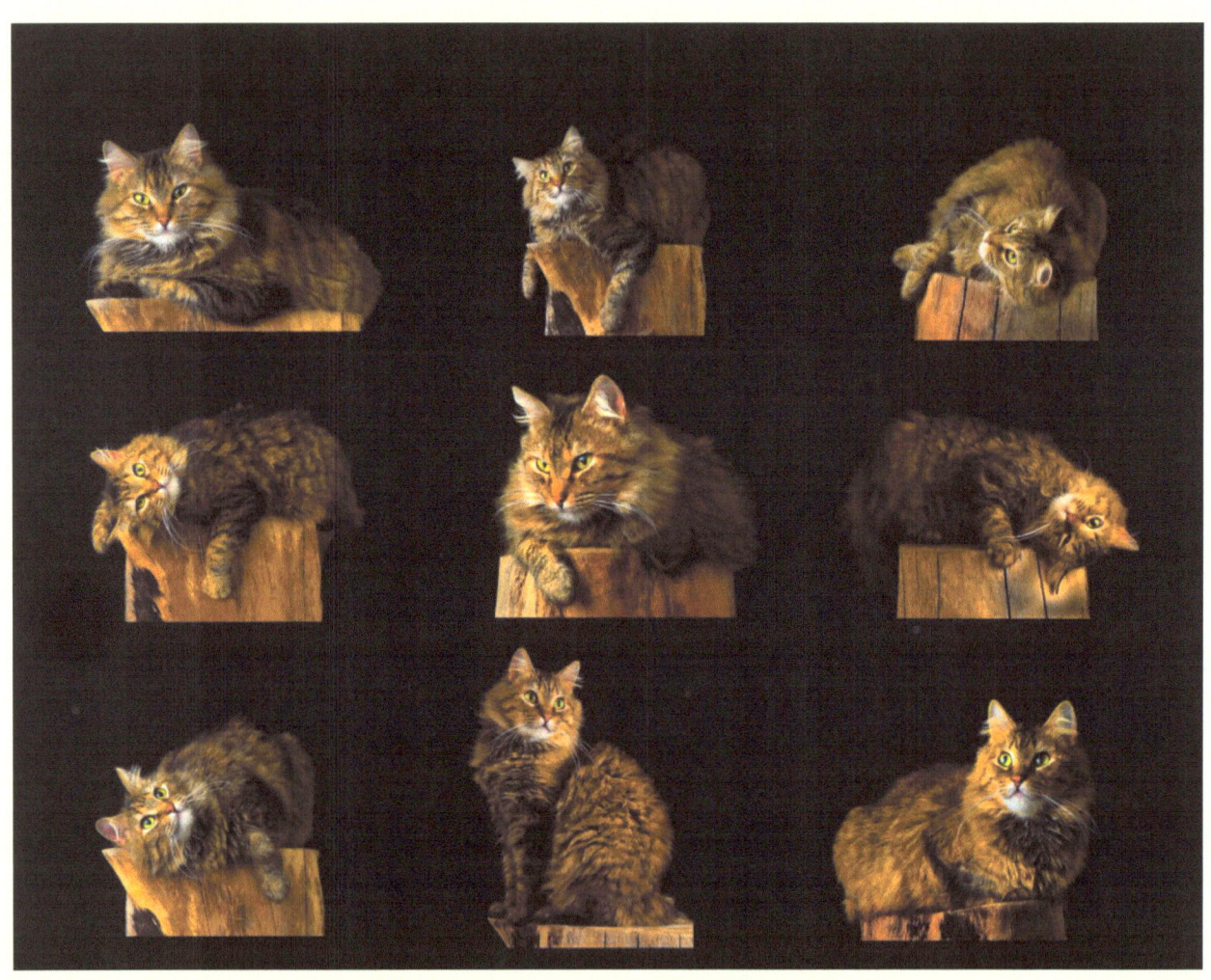

The cat persistently refuses to be categorized. She does not relinquish her mystery. This is why writers and artists have sought her company. Cats are thought provoking.

Ode to Panther in a Patch of Catnip

Panther, when his day is done

One less rat beneath the sun

Will make his way to favored glade

To loll in quietude and shade

And imbibe the savory fumes

Of catnip's fragrant blooms

But Panther, is that grove you're in

An inducement into feline sin

Is what parts your lips a grin

Or just an addled smile?

Will it make you infantile

Demented, dense and senile

Panther will you grope confused

And dazed within a dismal haze?

Or with your psychic sails unfurled

Will you navigate the world

Transit the galactic swirl

And chase nimble cosmic squirrels?

Will you roam celestial trails

Soar upon the solar gales

Will you approach the portals

Of those castles in the clouds

And pierce the mortal veil?

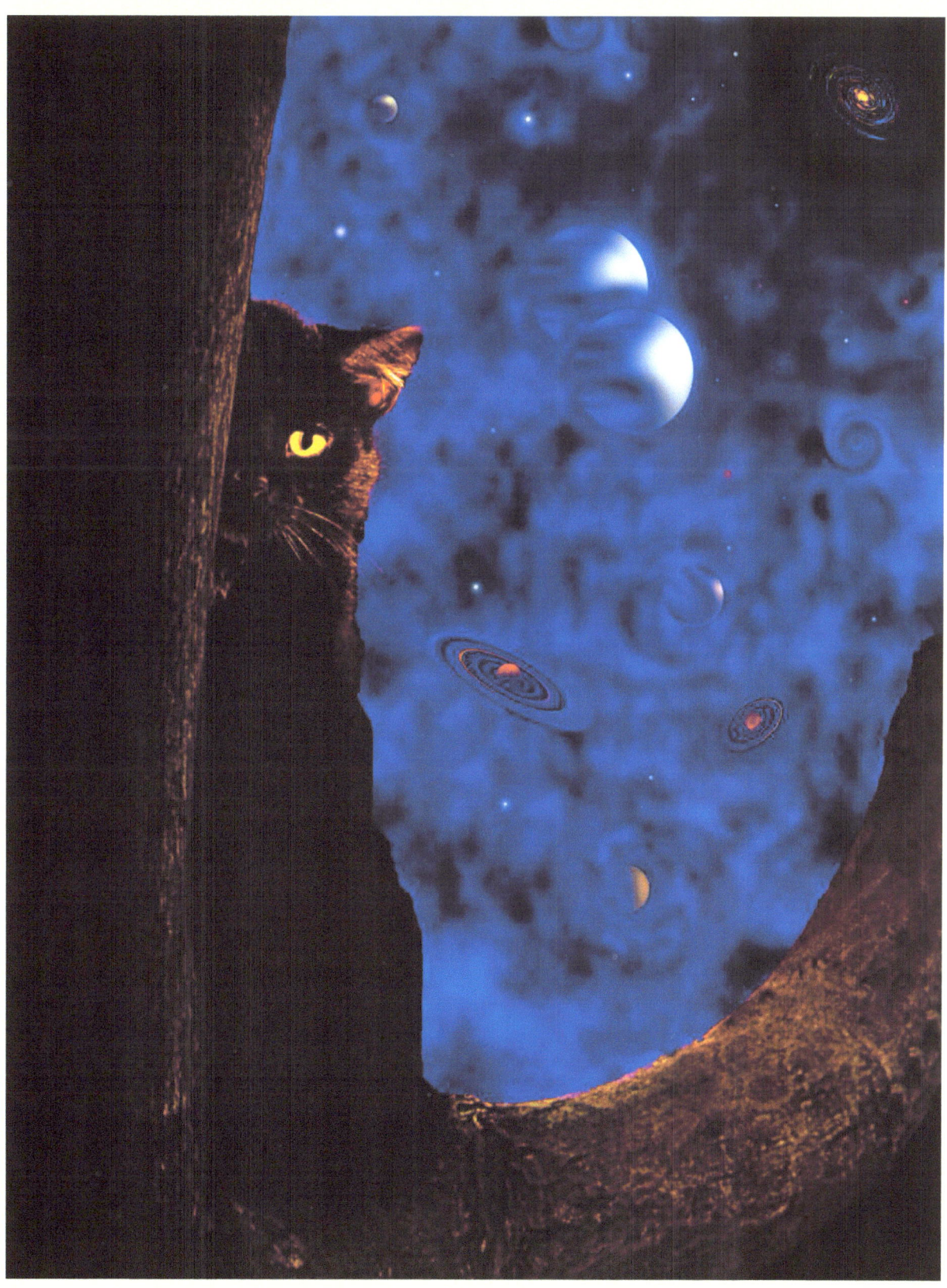

During the Middle Ages it was believed that the light from a cat's eyes came from within and that the cat made his way through the darkness with the aid, as it were, of a pair of feline headlights. This light was believed by some to be sunlight, which had been stored during the day. Others subscribed to the unnerving idea that the cat's eyes were portals through which shone the fires of hell.

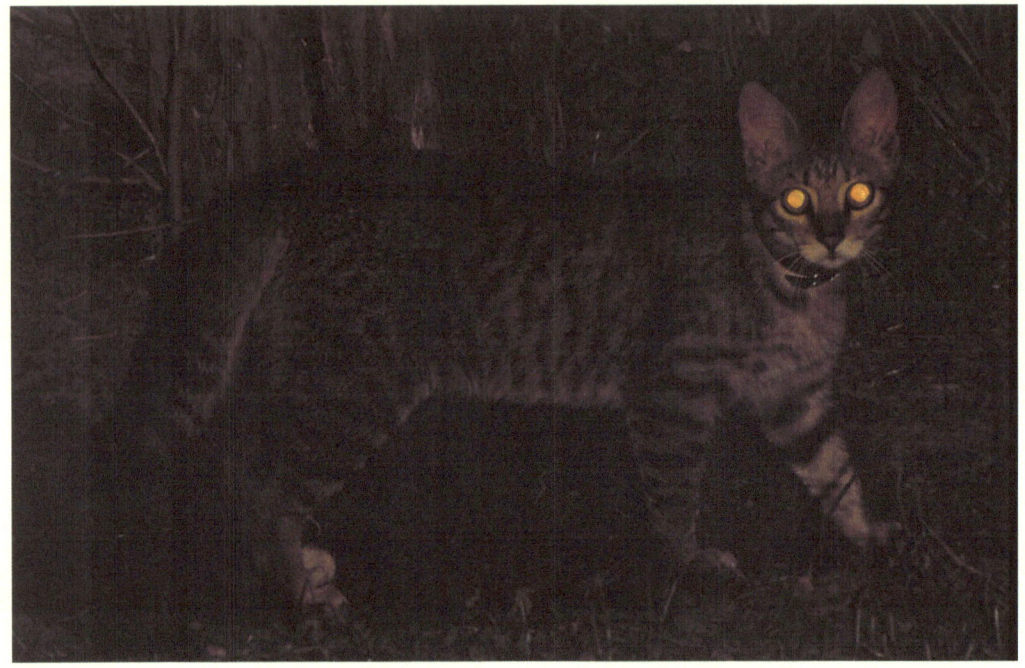

"In what distant deeps or skies burnt the fire of thine eyes?"

William Blake

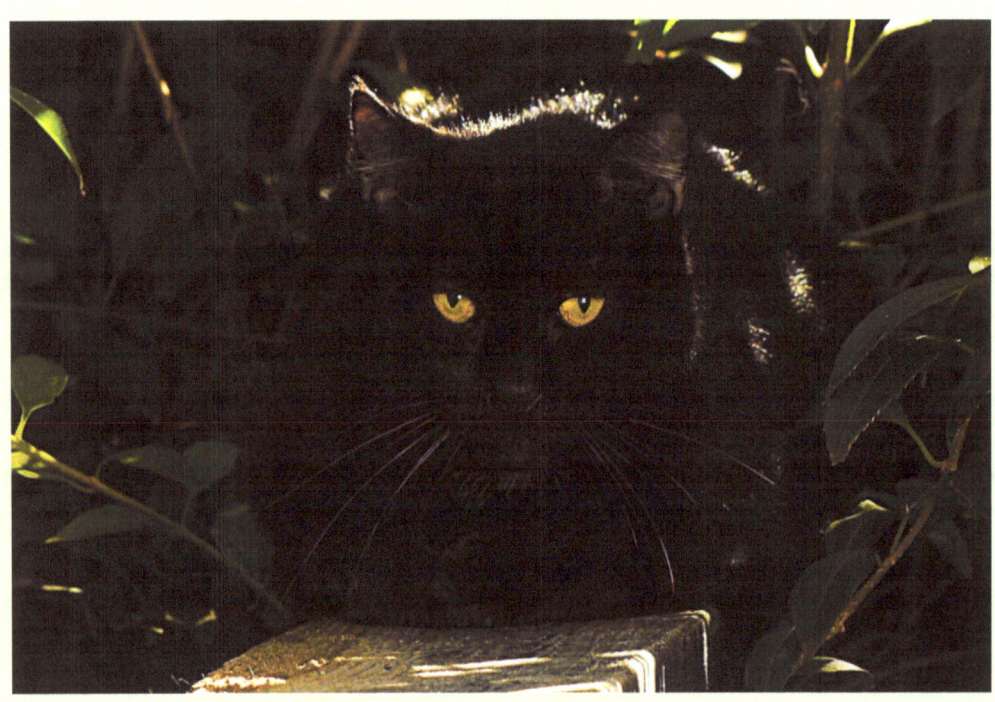

"...I am apt to treat him with respect from the idea he may be a great prince incognito, and may some time or other come to the throne." -Sir Walter Scott talking about his cat in a conversation with Washington Irving, 1817.

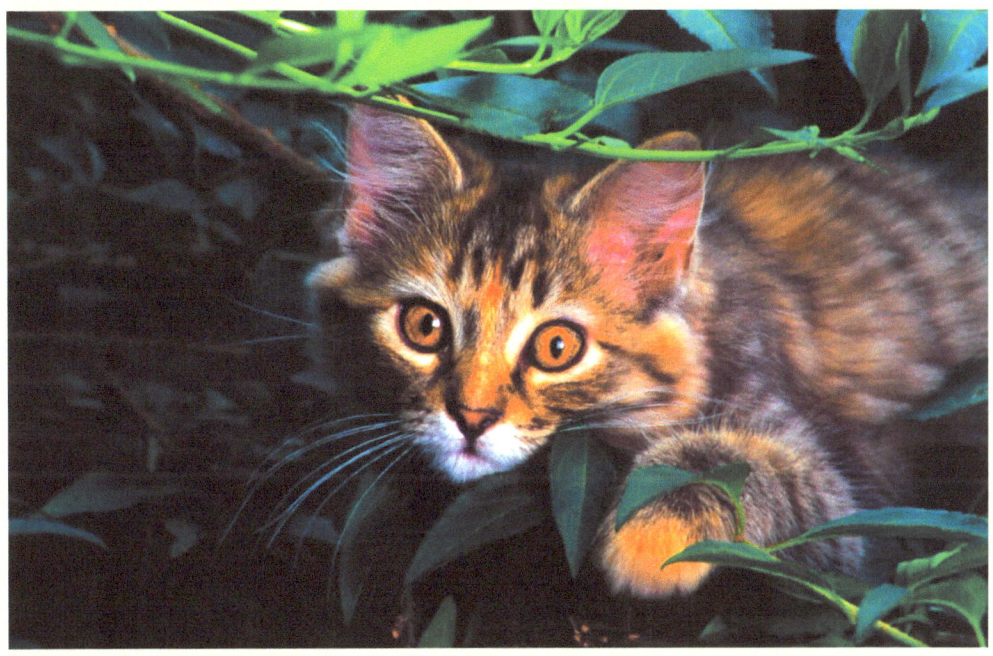

A cat dozing in the sun radiates a sense of serenity, an assurance that everything is in order, that the world is unfolding according to plan and that, in any event, he can handle whatever comes along.

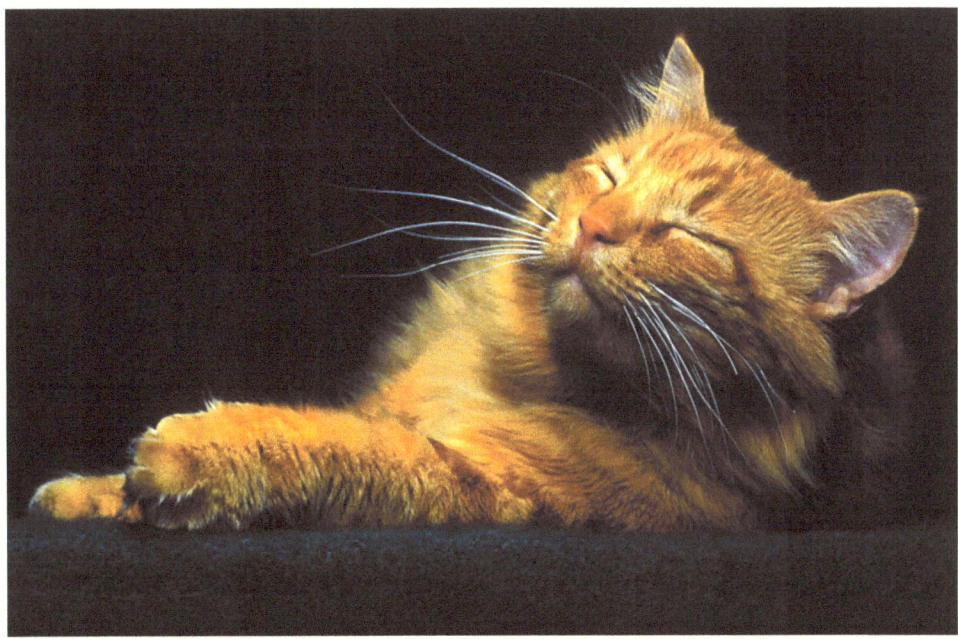

"Even in the dark ages the cat was the friend of the intelligent man, for the sorcerers and alchemists were the philosophers of the period and those who persecuted sorcerers and cats were the philistines."

Carl Van Vechten
Tiger Of The House

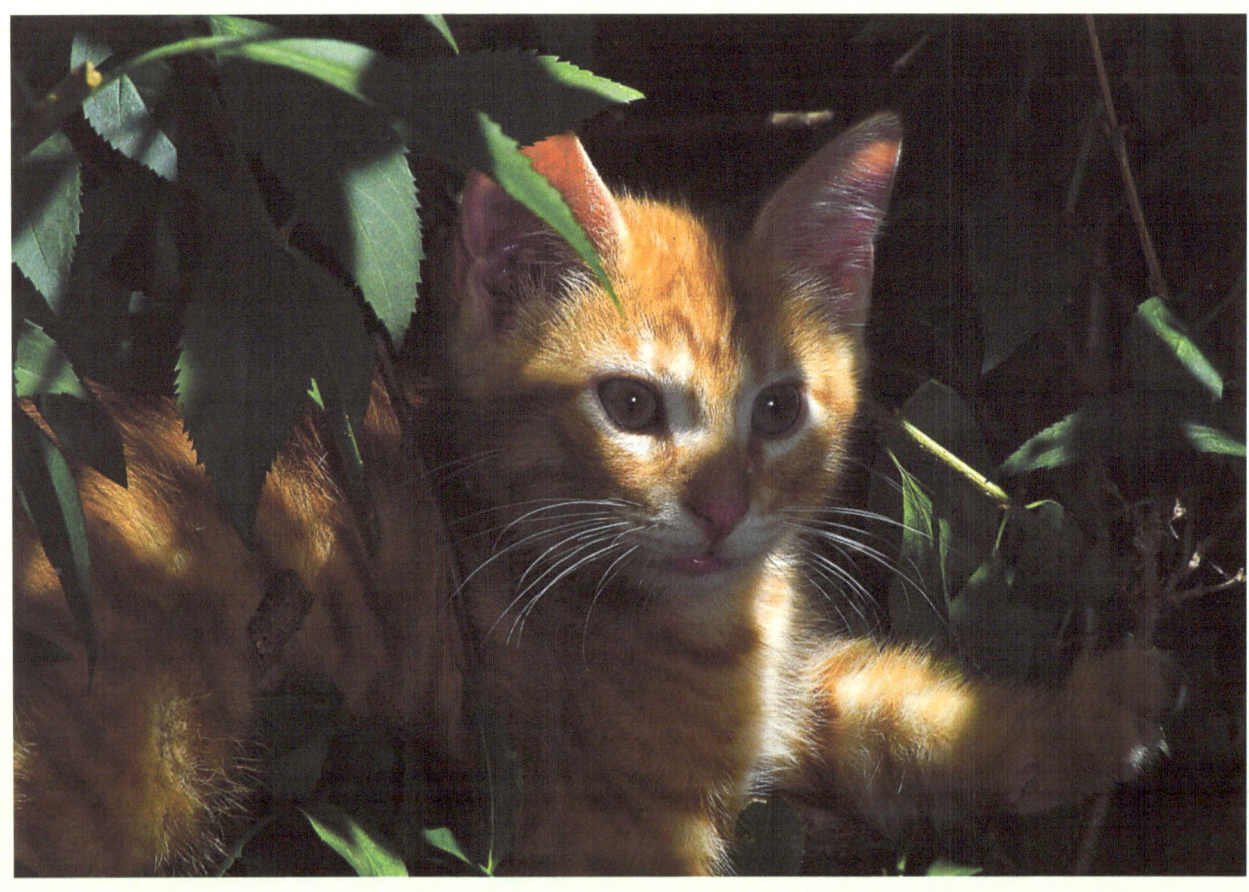

The cat and the dog are the only domestic animals for whom a place is reserved at the hearth, the only ones from whom companionship is as important a factor as their utilitarian qualities. They are the only animals that are customarily regarded as part of the family. They occupy complimentary positions. The dog is the companion of the hunt. The cat is the guardian of the threshold, destroyer of noxious vermin, protector of precious food supplies

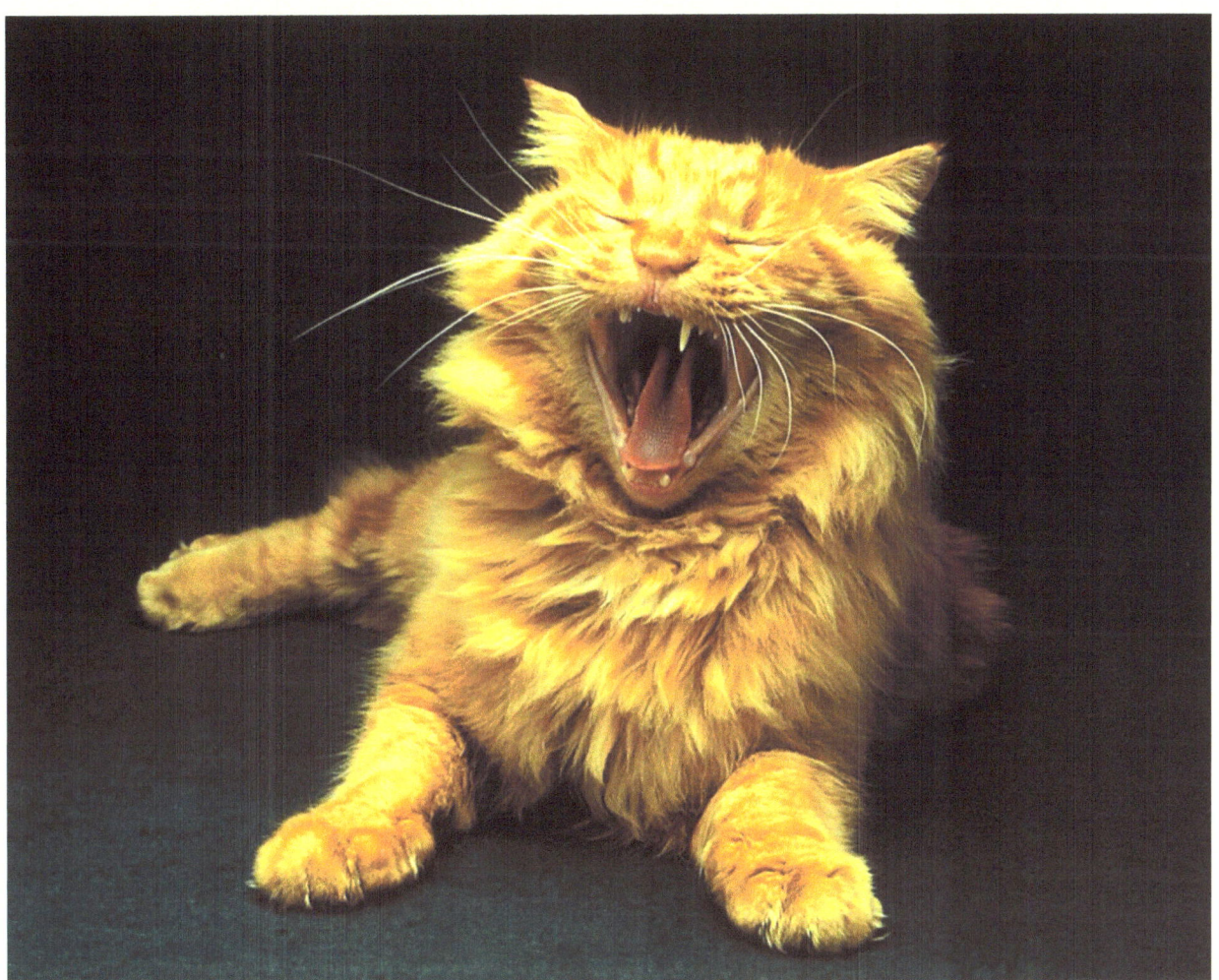

Despite their reputation for aloofness, cats have a genuine affinity for people. No other animal, except the dog, lives in such comfortable proximity to humans. Cats have found a niche between the human and natural worlds and they exploit it masterfully. Having evolved through cycles of feral and domestic states the cat, it seems, is keeping his options open.

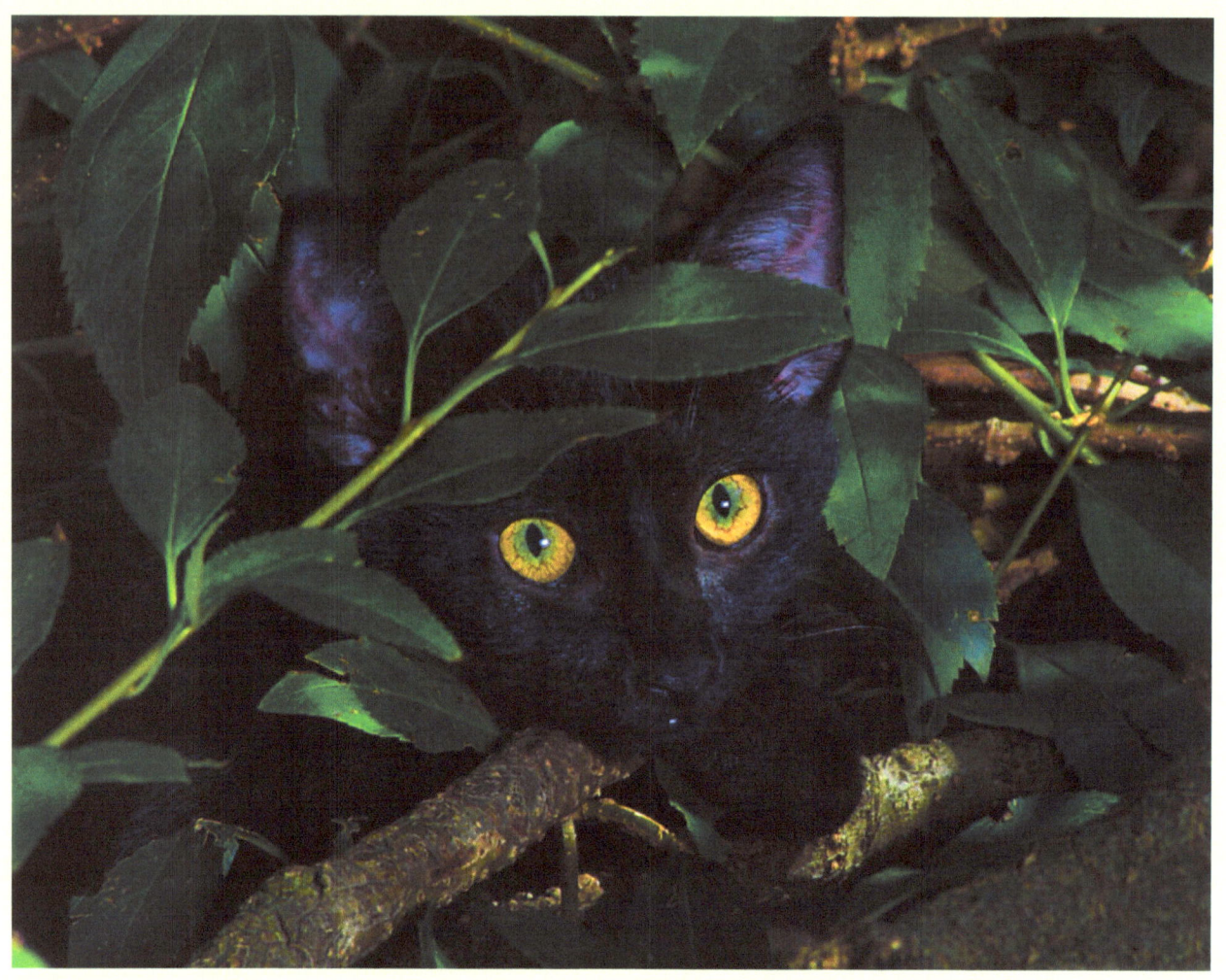

A Guardian of the Threshold

One evening after dinner Gustine, the cat, watched the sunset from the window of the farmhouse. It would have been pleasant to remain inside and watch the kittens performing acts of derring-do before the fire but Gustine had a job to do.

Gustine was a serious cat, somber and somewhat lugubrious. She was a philosopher. She was of the lithe and lean variety of cat but what she lacked in musculature she made up for in speed and many a cat had her nose boxed before she even knew what had happened. This was due to Gustine's being the queen of cats and her propensity for chastising those who failed to render due respect. With the title of queen, however, there came responsibilities, for Gustine was a metaphysical cat— a nocturnal cat, that is, who does battle with the demons of the night.

Gustine sat among a hedgerow overlooking a valley in which the town nestled a mile away and contemplated the difference between the wild and the settled life, then concluded that the distinction was moot as she had both. Alive to the sights, sounds and smells of the night, she was totally absorbed as if she were reading a book.

Gustine made her nightly rounds, peeking into the shadows, exploring all the nooks and hiding places in the grove. In time she came upon the fearsome Renfield, the king of cats, on his own nocturnal patrol. Gustine and Renfield, occasional consorts, touched noses and greeted each other with tranquil, euphonic trills. Renfield, a stern monarch, imposed a Draconian law on the neighborhood. Violators were prosecuted to the fullest extent under the statute of tooth and the ordinance of claw. Renfield was on the prowl for his rival, Durango, that malicious rascal who had recently shown signs of an intention to challenge Renfield's throne and upset the established order.

As the night deepened the darkness saw a stealthy shadow cross the glen, a form Gustine recognized as that of Lucifer's minion, Demogorgan, carrying a bag of tricks that he intended to sow among the townsfolk. The fallen angels, malignant spirits and assorted inhabitants of Hell were out tonight. Their machinations had been the subject of Gustine's investigations for many a season. As a philosopher, Gustine was dismayed by the relegation of demonology to the backwaters of theology. Being on familiar terms with many of the fallen angels, against whom she stood guard, Gustine knew that the science of the demon species, in their myriad guises, still had merit.

Out they came, issuing forth from some fissure in the ground – demons of hatred, ignorance, and hypocrisy traversing the valley heading towards town. Many of them Gustine had crossed paths with before. There was Ascaroth, a demon of spies and informers and Andras, the demon of discord. There were places, far from this outpost of the cosmic empire, she knew, where great battles were raging. Such as the sigma sector, where Aguares, Grand Duke of the Eastern region of Hell, commanding 30 legions and Buer, a second order demon who nonetheless commands 50 legions, were squaring off against an army of angels. Gustine guarded her threshold, an invisible perimeter that she maintained across which demons transgressed at their peril. It seemed as if they had chosen to look the other way tonight, rather than confront Gustine with her supernatural claws and metaphysical fangs. But then, as the cat sat in the glade, who should pass by but

Xaphan, a second order demon who keeps the fires of Hell stoked and blazing. At the time of the angels' rebellion, it was Xaphan's suggestion to set Heaven on fire.

"Good evening Gustine, it's been a while," said Xaphan.

"Xaphan," said Gustine, "I trust you've delegated your infernal duties to an able lieutenant."

"You can be sure of that, Gustine."

"And what brings you out tonight, your heinous?"

Behind a visage of smiling rage, he laughed quietly. "I'd love to tell you Gustine, but as Pascal opined, "ugly deeds are most estimable when hidden.""

"I can tell by your tone that something exceptionally malicious is afoot."

"Deliciously so, I'm afraid."

"Do you ever weary of sowing discord and destruction, Xaphan?"

"I used to," he said somewhat ruefully. "I used to be a distinguished gentleman, with all that that implies, but those days are over. Now, I must admit, I take a certain grim satisfaction in it all. It is, in the end, the roll I've been given. You do know that God is calling the shots in this show, don't you? He is, after all, omnipotent."

The toad-like apparition had such a disarming manner that she was tempted to engage in a little philosophical conversation. But as he stepped closer, Gustine felt her claws begin to unsheathe, and when the demon, covertly, crossed her perimeter, she sprang onto the beast, attaching herself to his leg, biting out pieces of flesh and sending him howling back into the night.

Gustine returned to her perimeter. In time the shadows faded and sunlight began to pierce the air. Gustine sat in the garden and welcomed the spirits of the morning.

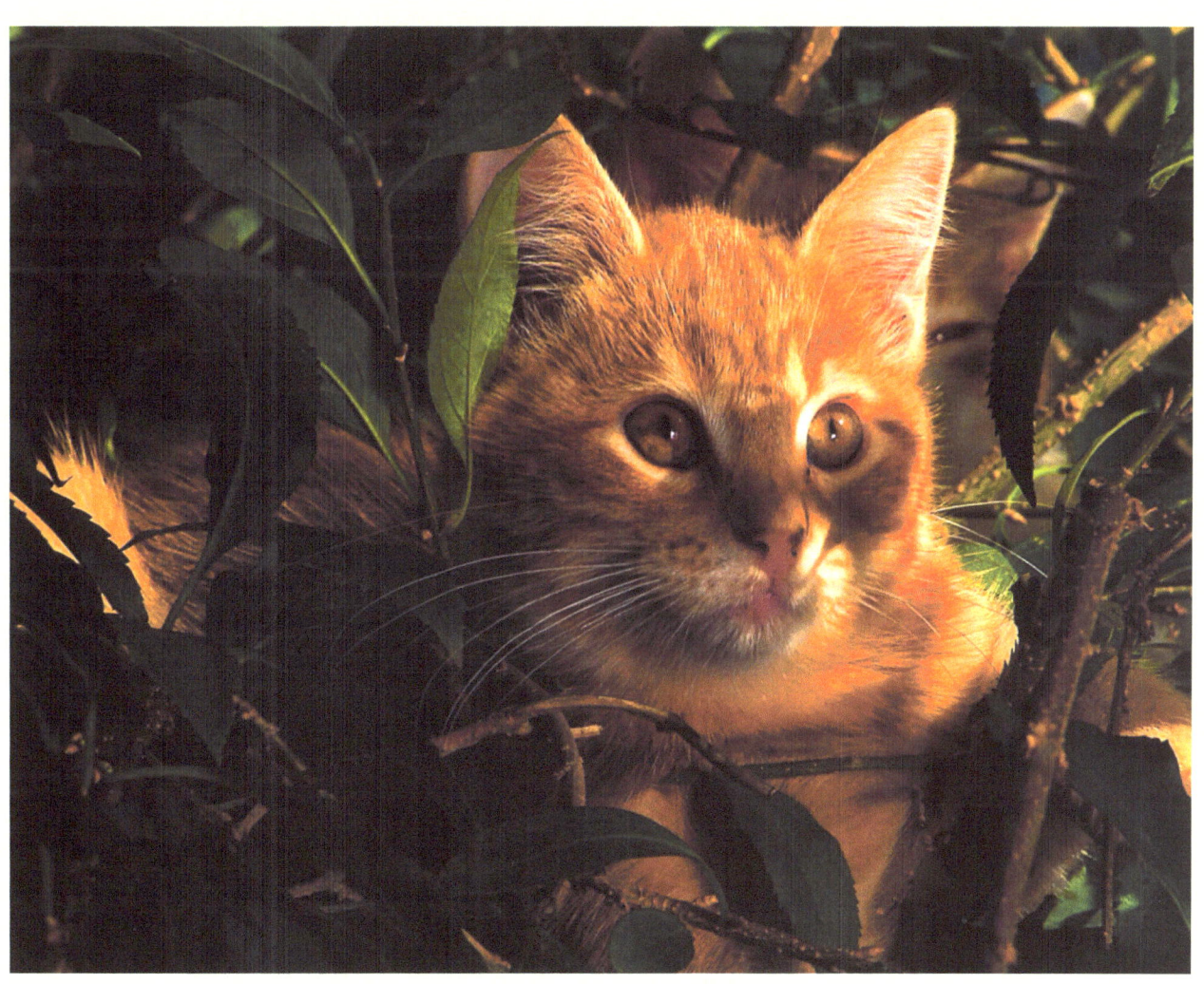

www.ingramcontent.com/pod-product-compliance
Lightning Source LLC
Chambersburg PA
CBHW050943200526
45172CB00020B/1058